TABLE OF CONTENTS

INTRODUCTION

Introduction

It's a dog's life and what a life to have especially if you happen to be a Shih Tzu. Just ask the owner of one of these loveable canines. Raising Shih Tzu can be a task in its' self, but it also can bring pure joy to those who own them.

Some are raised as "show dogs", but many people find their sunny disposition endearing and prefer to raise them as pets and companions. As a matter of fact, they are the perfect companion breed of dog because they adapt easily and tend to be a lively and happy dog. Shih Tzu are the perfect family dog.

They are also very popular with the dog show set because they are very easy to train and get along very well with other dogs. Shih Tzu who are bred for show only require higher maintenance than those who are raised as pets. Show Shih Tzu require more frequent grooming and overall care to stay in show condition.

Through this Ebook I hope to take you through the life cycle of these fantastic creatures. You will learn of the origin of Shih Tzu dogs, their physical characteristics, how to care for them properly, how to breed them, raise the pups and you will learn how to rescue them.

The information in these pages will take you into the world of owning a Shih Tzu. It will give you some insight into just what it takes to care for them properly so they can live a long and healthy life. It will also show you how much joy you can get from owning one. So sit back and relax and enjoy learning all about Shih Tzu.

History of the Shih Tzu Dog Breed

Modern DNA testing reveals that the Shih Tzu (pronounced shēd-zü or shēt sü) is one of the oldest breeds of dog in the world. Those who live with a Shih Tzu can easily imagine their regal, loyal little companions gracing the imperial palaces of ancient China.

Although historians disagree on the exact dates when the Shih Tzu breed emerged, they are generally believed to have descended from Tibetan dogs that were given to Chinese rulers as tribute. Once in China, these relatives of the Lhasa Apso may have been bred with the Chinese Pekingese to produce the Shih Tzu. The name Shih Tzu means "lion dog," and their long hair does resemble a mane and gives them a lion-like appearance.

Some scholars say Tibetan monks gave these dogs as gifts to Chinese rulers from during the Ming Dynasty (1368 to 1644); others point to a gift of these dogs from the Dalai Lama, Tibet's spiritual leader, to the Dowager Empress Tzu Hsi of the Manchu Dynasty in the late 1800s. However, similar dogs appear in paintings and art objects from the Tang Dynasty (618–907) and during a later period from 990–994, suggesting that the Shih Tzu were in China for centuries before these dates. Marco Polo, the famous Italian explorer who spent 17 years in China during the 1200s, reported seeing small "lion" dogs in the courts of Emperor Kublai Khan.

A Sacred Dog

Buddhists revere the Shih Tzu because they resemble lions, an important Buddhist symbol. Some people believe the Shih Tzu inspired the famous carvings of Fu Dogs that guard Buddhist Temples and remain popular statues today, often rendered in jade or porcelain. The Shih Tzu is also called the Chrysanthemum Dog because its hair radiates from its face like the petals of the flower. Asians have cultivated Chrysanthemums for some 2,000 years as an herb and the Chinese believed the plant contains the power of life.

One of many ancient legends tells how Siddhartha (who would later become the Buddha) traveled throughout India with a cheerful little dog at his side. When robbers surrounded him, his tiny companion changed into a roaring lion who so terrified the would-be robbers that they fled. After this strange incident the fierce lion reverted back into the small dog. Full of thanks, Buddha praised and kissed his small pet and blessed him for being so loyal and brave. According to this legend, white hair growing in the center of the forehead represents the place where Buddha laid his finger in blessing. Even today, many judges consider white on the forehead and tip of the tail to be favorable traits in Shih Tzu show dogs.

There may be some truth behind this legend. Siddhartha was born a prince, and although he abandoned earthly riches in his spiritual quest, noble families of his time period were known to breed toy dogs, so he could well have had a Shih Tzu for his traveling companion.

A Royal Breed

Whatever their mystic origins, experts agree that Shih Tzu were favorite palace playmates to the royal families of China. Bred as adored pets, they were a sign of wealth as they were not considered utilitarian. However, they were good watch dogs and their barking could alert the household to possible danger. Loyal to the entire noble family, they were friendly to strangers who were welcomed by members of the household—traits still evident in the modern breed.

Shih Tzu were prized then as now for their luxurious double coats of long hair. Today Shih Tzu come in almost any color combination. Empress Tzu His is said to have favored honey colored dogs with the Buddhist white splash on their foreheads.

Acceptance in the Modern World

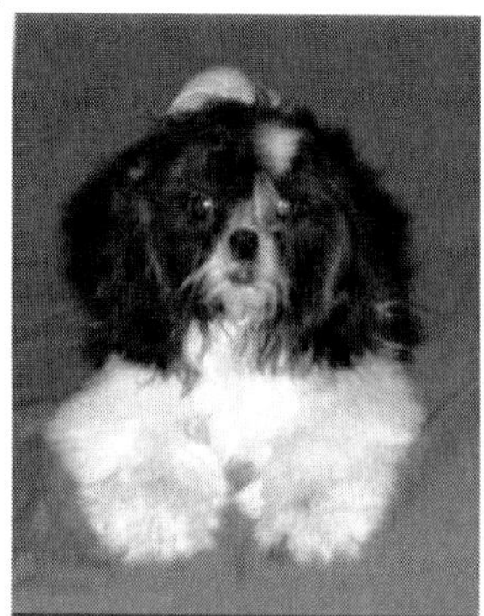

No matter when the Shih Tzu first appeared in China, it is a known fact that in the late 1800s the Empress Tzu His (already a dedicated breeder of Pekingese) eagerly added the rare dogs given to her by the Dalai Lama to her kennels, where their breeding was supervised by the palace eunuchs.

Some suspect that the eunuchs did not always follow her orders, or that breeding became haphazard after her death, so that interbreeding with Pekingese and Pugs occurred. As a result, identifying the breed became difficult.

When the last dynasty fell to the Chinese Revolution in 1911, many of the palace's Shih Tzu were destroyed during the violence. However, some survived. Years later the Peking Kennel Club formed in 1934. In 1938 it issued a breed standard for the Shih Tzu.

The Shih Tzu were introduced to the West in 1930 when Lady Brownrigg brought some to England, where they were at first classified as Lhasa Apsos. (Shih Tzu were also taken to Norway.) The Shih Tzu. Club of England formed in 1935. They were eventually recognized as a separate breed and granted their own register in 1940. Although some Shih Tzu found their way to America as early as the 1930s, they were extremely rare on this side of the pond until servicemen returning from WW II brought the popular dogs to the United States.

Ironically, this ancient breed is considered relatively "new" in the United States. It was not recognized by the AKC (American Kennel Club) as a separate breed until 1969, when it became the 116th recognized breed. The AKC requires six generations of pure breeding, so early mistaken crosses with Lhasa Apsos and an intentional cross with a Pekingese in England (the bowed legs of the Pekingese heritage can still be found in some Shih Tzu dogs) delayed their acceptance.

In 2004 the lovable Shih Tzu was the 9th most popular of the AKC's 153 recognized dog breeds. They are classified in the AKC's Herding group as a toy in the non-sporting dogs category.

Physical Characteristics of the Shih Tzu Breed

Size

Unlike some breeds, the Shih Tzu has a wide variation in acceptable standard sizes. Considered a toy breed, American Kennel Club standards describe an ideal mature Shih Tzu as weighing between 9 and 16 pounds and standing 9 to 10 ½ inches high at the withers (the ridge between the shoulder bones), and not less than 8 inches nor more than 11 inches. A Shih Tzu, they say, "must never be so high stationed as to appear leggy, nor so low stationed as to appear dumpy or squatty."[1]

Body Style

A Shih Tzu has a round head and dark, wide-set, intelligent eyes that look straight ahead. His heavily coated ears are large and sit a little below the crown. The Shih Tzu do not have wrinkled or down turned noses. Nostrils should be wide and open. Ideally, the Shih Tzu's muzzle should be no longer than one inch. His lower lip and chin neither protrude nor recede. With a broad, wide, undershot jaw, the Shih Tzu's teeth and tongue should not show when the mouth is closed.

A true Shih Tzu will be a compact, sturdy toy dog whose length is slightly longer than his height. The Shih Tzu's well-padded feet point straight ahead.

The luxurious double coats for which the Shih Tzu are famous come in a wide variety of colors and markings, all of which are considered standard and equally desirable, including gray, liver-colored, white, and black. A Shih Tzu's lips, eye rims and nose are black on all colors except they may be liver on liver-colored dogs or blue on blue pigmented dogs. The flowing hair may have a slight wave that is not considered a defect. A Shih Tzu's ears hang down, and her long hair can blend seamlessly into the coat on her body.

One of the Shih Tzu's most recognizable and beloved physical traits is her regal, heavily plumed tail, which sits high and curves over her back, lending an adorably arrogant air to the small dog's appearance. It is as though every Shih Tzu is remembering that they were once the cherished pets of the nobility who lived in splendid royal palaces.

Selecting Your Shih Tzu

If you have decided you have room in your heart for one of these adorable dogs—and room in your schedule for the necessary grooming and training—you'll want to begin searching for a reputable breeder who loves the breed and is more concerned about promoting and improving the breed as in making money

Choose a breeder who will allow you to see all the puppies in the litter, the mother, and the area where the puppies are living. Watch how the puppy you are considering interacts with the other dogs in the litter. A playful, energetic, sweet-tempered puppy is likely to be a healthy one. Pay attention, also, to the puppy's mother. Be sure she is also a healthy, obedient, intelligent and affectionate dog.

Finally, examine the puppy's living quarters. You'll want to purchase a puppy from a breeder who keeps the puppy's sleeping area clean. Dogs that are forced to eliminate in their sleeping areas or cages may lose their natural instinct to keep their "dens" clean, and you will lose a valuable tool for housebreaking your new companion.

Of course, you will want to select a puppy with a clean, healthy coat, firm, pink gums, white teeth, and eyes and ears that are free of foreign matter. You may also want to consider that a Shih Tzu with a silky coat will need less brushing and will be less likely to have tangles and mats than a Shih Tzu with a cottony textured coat.

The breeder should be glad when you tell him or her that you plan to take your new puppy to your veterinarian to be examined within the first couple of days after your purchase. Find out the breeder's policy (preferably in writing) on returning for refund or exchange a puppy that has a serious health issue.

Small dogs have long life spans, and you are making a big commitment by purchasing a Shih Tzu. You may want to observe the puppy you have chosen on several visits at different times of the day before making a final decision. A puppy who seems listless during one visit may simply be exhausted from energetic play; however, a puppy who is always tired may have a significant health problem.

Threats to the Breed

The rising popularity of the Shih Tzu breed has enticed some unscrupulous breeders to enter the market. You'll want to steer clear of these puppy mills. Beware of any breeder who shows you one animal by itself in a room that is separate from the living quarters of the other dogs. You have a right to ask to see the other puppies in the litter and the mother. Do they look healthy, clean, and well cared for? A good breeder will be able to tell you the history of the breed, answer your questions about care and training, and show you how to groom a Shih Tzu's luxurious hair.

In an attempt to cash in on the popularity of small breeds, some breeders have been crossing Shih Tzu with Toy Poodles to produce the Shih-poo. These dogs are often found in mass production kennels and pet stores. To be sure you are buying a true Shih Tzu, carefully study the AKC breed standard (see the link at the end of this book) and make sure the dog you are buying is a true representative of the breed. Not every Shih Tzu—not even the most glamorous show dog—will perfectly reflect every standard detail of the breed, but the standard will help you tell the difference between the Shih Tzu and similar toy breeds.

A true Shih Tzu is an excellent watch dog who will efficiently alert you when anyone comes to your door. Most owners consider this a very positive trait and the Shih Tzu himself definitely believes that he is earning his keep by his heroic vigilance. But poorly bred dogs can be yippy and snappish, so be careful and choosy when selecting your future companion.

Grooming and Caring for Your Shih Tzu

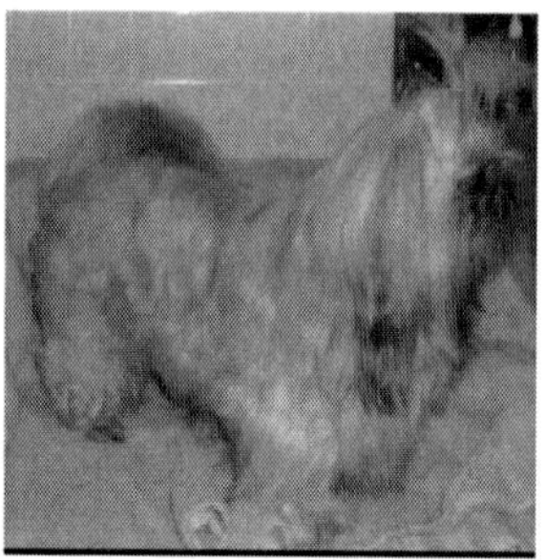

One reason Shih Tzu are so popular is for their luxurious, dense, flowing double coats. The long hair on their heads is often tied in an adorable top knot so they can see better and to show off the way they naturally carry their heads high. However, these stunning coats must be brushed every day, or at a minimum every other day. Some people will trim their Shih Tzu's hair short to simplify grooming. This is a better alternative than allowing a pet's hair to become matted and dirty, but doing so wastes one of the best features of the Shih Tzu.

The time you spend lovingly grooming your little dog will pay off in closer bonding and even more devotion from this naturally trusting and affectionate companion. You may fall in love with the Shih Tzu's flowing hair, but if you do not have time to spend bathing and brushing a long-haired dog, or the finances to pay for regular grooming, you would be happier if you adopted a different breed. If you purchase your Shih Tzu for rowdy romps in the backyard (which she will enjoy), you will need to groom her even more frequently to keep her hair free of tangles and matting. Still, a Shih Tzu requires less grooming than some other long-haired dog breeds.

Start Your Grooming Ritual Early

Begin brushing your Shih Tzu puppy daily—even if only for a couple of minutes and even if his immature coat doesn't really need to be brushed—and you will establish the brushing habit for both of you. Make this a time of closeness and gentle care and you will be rewarded by years of loyal friendship from your Shih Tzu. This is also a great job for older children, if you train them how to properly groom your Shih Tzu, and will teach a loving child valuable lessons in patiently nurturing and caring for another living being.

Some Shih Tzu owners report that at about 10 to 12 months of age, a Shih Tzu's coat will change. You may become discouraged in your brushing because mats may seem to form faster than you can untangle them. Fortunately, this condition is only temporary and lasts about three weeks to one month.

Bathing and Brushing Tips

Mats usually occur because the dead hair that naturally falls out gets knotted in the dog's long hair. Be sure to remove the mats before you bathe your Shih Tzu. Since dirty coats mat more quickly, you'll want to give your Shih Tzu a bath at least once every two weeks, and once a week is better. To remove tangles, saturate them for a few minutes with cream conditioner. Don't rip or tear the mats out; instead carefully separate the strands of hair.

Never brush a totally dry coat. If you aren't bathing your dog, you can use a spray bottle to dampen the hair, brushing from the ends to the roots and working from the bottom up.

Placing a towel on the bottom of the sink when bathing your Shih Tzu will give him the feeling of having more secure footing while bathing. Placing your hand under your dog and holding him securely with one hand, soak him with lukewarm water, shampoo his body, and rinse thoroughly. Then wet his head and clean his topknot using no-tear shampoo. You'll find a wide variety of shampoos and dog grooming aids at a well-stocked pet store. When bathing your Shih Tzu, be careful not to get water in his up-turned nose. And don't forget to clean the inside corners of his eyes with a damp washcloth soaked in warm water.

After his bath, cuddle him in a dry towel to make him feel secure and to help his thick coat dry more quickly. You may want to use a small handheld blow dryer on the lowest setting to dry his coat, being careful to keep the blast of air away from his large, sensitive eyes. Gently clean your Shih Tzu's ears with a cotton swab dipped in mineral oil, being careful not to push the tip too far into the ear, which could injure the delicate eardrum.

Creating That Cute Topknot

When you finish bathing and brushing, you'll be ready for the most enjoyable part of grooming—giving your Shih Tzu a charming topknot. Some people choose to braid their Shih Tzu's long hair, or make artistic top knots in elaborate patterns set off with beautiful bows. If you are a beginner, you'll want to start with a simple, single top knot. Your Shih Tzu will need to wear his topknot every day to keep the hair out of his face and eyes.

When making the topknot, use only elastic bands that do not break hair (you can purchase these from an orthodontist, a pet supply store, or at a dog show). When removing the elastic, cut the bands with scissors. Never pull them out as this could be painful and also could cause the hair to break. As a Shih Tzu puppy grows into an adult, the facial hair will grow longer and longer, allowing you to create more elaborate and beautiful topknots as your skill increases.

Shih Tzu Have Personality Plus

Even if Shih Tzu were not such beautiful dogs people would still prize them as pets because of their wonderful personalities. Just like the beloved palace pets in ancient China, your Shih Tzu will befriend every member of your household and the visitors you accept. Like us humans, every Shih Tzu is an individual with a distinct personality, but in general, they are playful but not high strung, friendly to anyone who is accepted by the family, loving with children who do not play with or handle them too roughly, and can be content in an apartment or with a small yard.

Shih Tzu can become spoiled and love to be the center of attention, so they may be indignant at the interest babies or toddlers receive. But Shih Tzu can be perfect companions for older children, especially if the children are willing to help with exercise, grooming and feeding. Shih Tzu will usually get along well with other pets. Cheerful and intelligent, they are generally affectionate and loyal, thriving on your loving attention as they enjoy snuggling with you. They are fun to watch as they walk proudly around your palace. Bred for centuries to be companions and pets, it is no wonder the breed has soared in popularity and become one of the most sought-after dogs in the toy group.

Training Your Shih Tzu

Although some Shih Tzu can be a little too independent, strong-willed and difficult to train, most owners report that their Shih Tzu dogs respond well to gentle but firm teaching methods. The breed's natural intelligence helps them grasp what you are teaching them quickly, and more than compensates for their occasional stubbornness. They do not respond well to punishment. You will find rewards and praise to be much more effective training methods. As with all dogs, patience and consistency, as well as investing the necessary time in training, will reap years of rewards in a well-behaved companion who is a delight to everyone in the household.

Housebreaking

Just as parents of toddlers struggle with potty training, perhaps no aspect of training your Shih Tzu to be a welcome member of your household is more vital than successful housebreaking. Every child responds to different methods—for example, some are motivated by sticker charts and rewards while others could care less about such gimmicks but are desperate to wear "big kid" underwear—so don't expect your Shih Tzu to respond to the exact training methods that worked wonders for another dog in a different household. By all means, listen to all the advice you can get and try the methods that you think might work for you and your dog, but don't be discouraged if the fool-proof method you read about in a magazine doesn't work like magic on your little friend.

Adapt the best ideas for your personality and your dog's, and remember to be patient. It can take months to train human children in the preferred methods of elimination, and your Shih Tzu will most likely master the concept much more quickly.

Two of your biggest allies in the campaign to teach your Shih Tzu to use the approved area for elimination are:

1. His natural desire to keep his den clean and;
2. His desire to please you, the leader of his pack, and earn your enthusiastic praise and attention.

One of the most popular methods of training a dog is crate training.

Some dog owners abhor the thought of confining their dogs in a kennel crate, and dogs can be successfully trained without using one.
However, for many dog owners, especially those who must be gone from the home for several hours to work, they can be lifesavers (and furniture savers and shoe savers . . .).

First-time dog owners are often pleasantly surprised at how quickly their dogs take to their crates and how much they enjoy spending time there. Many if not most dogs have a natural desire for a safe den.
However, a dog crate must be used properly to be effective and humane.

You want your Shih Tzu to consider her crate as her own personal den.
<u>It should never be used to punish the dog.</u>

Most likely, if you position the crate in an area of your home that is near the action and leave the door open, your dog will often visit her crate on her own just to hang out and feel safe, especially if she is feeling overwhelmed by too much activity or noise in the household.

You can place treats and toys in the den for her to discover, thus reinforcing the crate as a positive place, but most dog parents find this is not necessary.

If you don't have a crate or don't care to use one, you can use baby safety gates to confine your dog in a kitchen or large bathroom or other area in your home that would be easy to clean in case of accidents and that is free of hazards such as electric cords.

If you are going to paper train your Shih Tzu, be sure to place the newspaper (or commercial puppy training pads) as far away from his food and sleeping area as possible in the confined area.

Be sure your Shih Tzu has had ample opportunity to eliminate outside or in the approved area before you confine him to the crate.

In the early weeks this will mean your going outside with him several times a day.

If you stay in the house and shove him out the door, he may be so upset at being separated from you that he will not concentrate on the "job" he needs to do. It will take time for him to learn to go outside on his own, and what is expected of him once there.

Every time you go outside, speak a simple command, such as, "Outside" or "Let's go." Use that command only for going outside to eliminate and soon your dog will know what you expect when you say the command.

Gradually he will be confident enough to go outside to do his business on his own without having to worry that you have abandoned him.

Many dog owners will reward their dogs with treats when they successfully eliminate outdoors. However, this can backfire with the intelligent Shih Tzu, who may be so excited about the treat he knows you have in your pocket or that you'll give him when you go back inside that he can't concentrate on the task at hand.

Your dog appreciates being able to "go to the bathroom" when he needs to as much as you do, and your lavish praise is probably all the reward he will need.

When you go outside with your Shih Tzu, don't rush her. She may need to sniff several spots before she finds the perfect spot for her purposes.

This can be quite humorous (unless the weather is bad, which never seems to speed up the process). In fact, she may feel the need to select two, three or four "perfect" spots and circle around each several times during one visit to the yard. If you hurry her, she may not completely eliminate and may have an accident soon after reentering the house.

Many dog trainers say dogs will learn to use a certain type of surface for elimination—and you want your dog to prefer grass or paper over carpet. Taking them to the same area in the yard will reinforce the idea that this-is-where-you-go because he will smell areas where he has done so in the past.

Taking your dog outside on a schedule is also recommended. Dogs like the secure familiarity of a routine and can better learn to control their bladder and bowels when they know what to expect.

Don't expect your Shih Tzu to be perfect in his housebreaking. He may have several successful days of staying clean and yet still have accidents.

Pay close attention to your young dog. If you catch her in the act of going in the house, make a noise, such as firm "NO!" to startle her, which will often make her stop in mid stream.

Immediately take her outside and encourage her to finish the job, praising her in your most positive and loving tones if she goes outside or even attempts to do so.

Another method of discouraging her is the "water bottle" method.

Keep a spray bottle containing clean water handy. When you catch her in the act, simply (discreetly. You don't want to let her know you're the one responsible) give a little squirt of water. Again, take immediately outside.

When your Shih Tzu has an accident in the house, be sure to clean the area immediately and spray it with one of the commercial products that neutralize the smell (or spray a mixture of vinegar and water on the spot).

If you do not remove the smell, your dog may logically assume that place is an approved area for elimination and may visit it the next time nature calls.

Rubbing your dog's nose in the mess or beating her with a newspaper are less than successful methods and often lead the sociable Shih Tzu to become obstinate, resentful and distrustful.

Remember that your little friend wants to please you and that young dogs have great difficulty in learning to control their internal plumbing.

Don't assume an episode of eliminating indoors is an act of defiance. It was more likely due to a larger than usual meal, not being taken outside on schedule, having drunk more water than usual due to warm weather, or a similar no-fault reason.

Above all, remember that housetraining does not happen overnight. It requires loving patience. Investing the proper time in training early will pay off later in a well-trained companion.

Crate Training

When considering using the crate training method of housebreaking your Shih Tzu, there are several facts that you will need to keep in mind. For instance, because of a lack of physical maturity, young pups cannot hold their bodily functions it for very long. Secondly, many owners provide too large of a crate for the pup's size giving him too much room to move around in.

Take the dog out of the crate after naps, before bedtime or when you return home after being away. Take him out to potty regularly at those specific times. You need to be disciplined to do this consistently.

As a matter of fact, when he is out of his crate, you need to take him out to potty often, especially after feedings or napping.

Whenever the dog is out of his haven (crate), he will need to be watched ***constantly*** to avoid any "accidents" in the house.
The more the puppy is taken out to potty and returned to his crate, the quicker he will get the idea that the only place he can potty, is outside.

One of the downfalls of owning a Shih Tzu is the difficulty some owners have with housebreaking them.
It doesn't happen with all Shih Tzu however, it does happen more often than not. In fact, many Shih Tzu puppies even have difficulty with both crate training and liter box training.

One reason for the failure of these types of training is that owners only follow the process partially or sporadically.
And/or, give up too soon. Shih Tzu tend to take a little longer than most dogs.

To begin crate training first you provide him with a safe "haven" (the crate or an exercise pen). Once he learns to love his haven, then he will most likely want to keep it clean. He is not likely to mess the place that he sleeps in. That's the main premise behind crate training.

My Shih Tzu barks in his crate.

If you choose to crate train your Shih Tzu but he barks and cries when the door is shut at night, the crate might be too large, making him feel insecure.

It should be large enough for him to turn around comfortably in, but not so large that he could pee in a corner away from where he is sleeping.

You can make his crate the correct size by cutting a piece of heavy cardboard to serve as a wall in the crate, moving it back as he grows. Also, placing an old afghan (or other covering that allows good air circulation) over the sides and back of the crate can also make him feel more secure.

Some dogs bark in their crates because they feel abandoned. You may want to place the crate in your bedroom so he can be near you.
Speaking lovingly and quietly to him will often calm and reassure him enough so that he can go to sleep.

Yelling harshly will usually just increase his anxiety and encourage him to bark more. Be sure you aren't leaving your Shih Tzu in his crate too long. Your vet can advise you as to how long your dog can be expected to stay clean in his crate at his particular stage of development.

Another possibility for a dog's barking in the crate is that he did not get enough exercise during the day. When you take your dog for daily walks, play throwing and retrieving games and enjoy other active pastimes, he will be much more like to fall contentedly asleep at night.

Exercise is as vital for your dog's health and well being as it is for yours.

Finally, having a daily routine will help your dog relax enough at night to sleep in his crate. Even if you don't follow a schedule yourself, try to establish a routine for meals, playtime, going outside, and going to bed so your Shih Tzu will know what to expect and will feel secure and have less reason to "complain" by barking.

Litter box training

If you choose the litter box method of housebreaking your Shih Tzu, you will first need to purchase an exercise pen for his confinement. You need to show him that he has a designated confined living area so to speak.

Once confined in the pen, you will need to make sure it is lined with plenty of newspaper or have a litter box put in the pen. This method of housebreaking a Shih Tzu is especially good for those owners that are away from home at least a few hours a day.

Since the thought of having a litter box for Shih Tzu appeals to owners more than the though of using newspapers, I will focus on the best way to introduce a litter box into the exercise pen where your Shih Tzu will stay. First things first, when I talk about a litter box, I don't mean a cat's litter box filled with cat litter. I mean creating a litter box out of a larger plastic bin with a squared off U-shaped opening cut out to make it easy for the dog to go in and out. Don't cut too far down or the litter will spill out and make a mess.

Next, fill the bin with a natural litter (never cat litter) such as "CareFresh" or "Yesterday's News." They're made of recycled newspaper. They're safe, non-toxic, dust-free, and environmentally friendly. You'll find them at pet supply stores. Make sure to place the bin in the pen where access will not be restricted.

When your Shih Tzu uses the litter box, make sure to praise him well. He will love this and most likely use it whenever he needs to while in the pen. One note here, only use the litter box for those times that you will be away from home for long periods of time. In conjunction with the litter box method of training, you will still need to train the dog to go potty outside.

It will be a time consuming process, but with consistency and perseverance, within a few months, you'll hit the jackpot when your Shih Tzu is completely trained. (Despite what you may have read or heard, you **cannot** housebreak your Shih Tzu in a weekend! One of our customers did have her puppy broken in a week. An excellent job on her and the puppys part.)

Now, here are some things that you should **never** do while attempting to housebreak your Shih Tzu.

- **Never** rub his nose in it if he has an accident in the house. Instead, clean it up and use an odor neutralizer, you can also use white vinegar on the spot to eliminate the odor and prevent him from returning to that spot for another accident. (A repellent such as "Keep-Off" works well)
- **Never** scold him if he has an accident, it won't do any good and may only confuse him because they forget easily and won't remember doing it.

Eventually your Shih Tzu will develop his own signal for when he needs to go out to potty. By closely observing your Shih Tzu during training, you will soon learn what these signals are and will be able to react in time. When your Shih Tzu does have to go out to potty, he may whimper, whine, bark or give some other sign that this is what he needs to do.

When your Shih Tzu does go potty outdoors, make sure to praise him well. He will love the fact that you seem so happy about what he just did and will try to repeat it again and again, just to get the praise. It definitely provides an incentive for your Shih Tzu to do it right.

A Valuable Housebreaking Tool

I call this my "***secret weapon***".

If you have a spare room near the back of the house, it may be a good idea to install a doggy door to allow your Shih Tzu to go outdoors to potty whenever he has a need.

The room would have to be one that holds little importance to you because you will need to confine your Shih Tzu to this area as his living quarters. By providing direct and constant access to the backyard, he is more likely to housebreak easier than with other methods.

This has been one of the best investments I've made. Especially considering we have four dogs. The dogs learn quickly to use it and enjoy the freedom of coming and going as they please. And, it saves me the trouble of getting up and letting them out. Personally, I would never be without one. (Remember: only use if your yard is "escape proof".)

Some people think this can't be done if they don't have a fenced yard but we are very imaginative and actually installed a doggie door in our camper.

We have a camping lot in Indiana with a camper and a deck, no fenced yard of course.
We used lattice to make sure our deck was escape proof because our male (Jake) is an escape artist. (We probably should have named him Houdini).
We also bought some yard gates for dogs that we secured to the ground so they could get off the deck and do their business.

We later switched the yard gates to a small fenced in area because a lot of bigger dogs were running loose in the campground and they could easily jump our yard gates even if our dogs were secured.

We also used lattice at one time to keep the dogs confined to the patio at our home because we were having our yard landscaped. (Which had the added effect of keeping tracked in mud to minimum).
So, even if your yard is not fenced there are alternative solutions you can use and install a doggie door. Just make sure, ***what ever you do***, make it escape proof because Shih Tzu can squeeze through small spaces.

Leash Training

When training your dog to accept a leash, it may be best to allow the dog to get used to the collar first. Let the dog wear the collar for a few days alone, then attach the leash to it and take him outdoors.

Make sure that the leash is long enough to give the dog plenty of room to run and jump, especially if you take him to play in a park or large open area.

Since Shih Tzu love companionship, and yours will certainly love spending time walking with you outdoors.

The trick with walking the dog on a leash is to never pull or tug the dog while walking. He will need to be taught how to walk with you without you having to keep pulling on the leash to pull him back.

Start the leash training by attaching a leash to the dog's collar. Drop the leash to the floor and let the dog drag it around for awhile. Call your dog to you and praise him when he comes. Make sure to leave the leash on for only a short time though and never when he is alone. Try this little trick several times a day for a few days and in no time, your dog will not even know the leash is there.

Next, take the dog outdoors, preferably in your yard (where there won't be any distractions) with the leash on and try walking around with the dog. Begin by making the dog "sit" next to where you are standing. Say the words "let's go" and take a step forward with your left foot.

Make sure to always begin with the left foot. You want to instill in the dog that this is his cue to move also. Walk at a normal pace, not too slow or too fast for either of you.

While you are both walking, stop at short intervals, praise the dog each time you stop, telling him what a good boy he is. Again, this will please him because he thinks that he is pleasing you by doing this. Also, he will enjoy it and associate it with something that is pleasant and fun. He will most likely want to repeat this often.

Health Issues You Should Be Aware Of

Tooth Care

It is very important that your Shih Tzu gets regular care to keep his teeth healthy (he may start to lose teeth by age seven). Improper or poor dental care is the number one health problem for all types of dogs, so it is important to start proper dental care while they are pups.

Regular dental care is essential in order to prevent early tooth loss and bladder or kidney infections. Use a toothbrush often to keep tartar down. It may be a good idea to ask your vet for instructions on properly brushing the teeth.

Professional scaling (cutting the teeth down) is essential as part of the regular dental care routine and your vet can show you how it's done. You can also do scaling at home if you prefer. A professional cleaning, scaling and polishing should be done once a year at the veterinary clinic. Cleaning of the teeth is important to prevent gingivitis, which is an inflammation of the gums caused by hardened plaque called "tarter."

NOTE: <u>NEVER use human toothpaste</u> to clean the teeth! Always buy special toothpaste and brushes from your vet or pet store.
You can also feed your Shih Tzu food that has a formula to aid in keeping plaque to a minimum.

Teeth problems

Improper bites and retained teeth are two of the problems that may appear in pups. Also, a “bad bite” may appear because the lower jaw juts out too far, or an “overbite” can occur if the upper jaw is too long.

The vet should have a look at any problems that arise with the teeth. Remember that the loss of the “baby teeth” is not that important. It is the loss of the permanent teeth that will pose a problem.

Early tooth loss can occur to any type of dog because of their physical makeup. For instance, genetics plays a big part in how long a dog will retain its teeth.

For one thing, the composition of the saliva in dogs differs from dog to dog. Additionally, if the dog has a shallow jaw, the teeth will have less bone to hold the teeth in place, which may result in early loss of teeth. Avoid wet foods that will stick to the teeth speeding up the plaque process.

You can also buy a variety of toys designed to help clean the teeth. Many of these toys massage the gums while the dog is chewing on them.

A good “rawhide” chew toy will do the trick provided that it doesn’t contain any harmful elements. Dogs, like humans also get bad breath. This could be the first indication that gingivitis is present (or some other disease). Make sure to examine the teeth and gums carefully to look for signs of redness or swelling of the gums.

If you notice a brown or yellow crust on the teeth, then you can be sure that plaque is building up or worse, it could be tarter. Look for any loose or broken teeth and have them taken care of immediately. With proper dental care, your dog can live a healthier life.

Ear Care

It is very common for dogs and cats to get occasional ear infections. Many Shih Tzu are particularly prone to excessive "build-up" in the ear which leads to infection.

Removal of excess ear hair is part of the ear cleaning routine. Remove the hair from the ear canal opening by pulling it with your fingers, or with hemostats. If you use hemostats you must be very careful not injure the dogs ear.

Talk to your vet about proper ear cleaning techniques and products. Check your Shih Tzu ears regularly and keep them clean.

Infections can occur in the outer part of the ear canal, the middle ear or the inner ear. Treatment includes thorough ear cleansing/cleaning, and appropriate doses of antibiotics may be needed.

If the dog suffers from food allergies, talk to your vet about changing his diet. (Here again, poor Millie has a terrible problem with her ears. While CiCi and Jake's ears require very little attention, Millies' need to be washed 2-3 times a week).

There are several good products available. Just ask your vet and I'm sure he'll have one he recommends.

Eye Care

(Tearing and Staining)

The main problems that appear with the eyes of a Shih Tzu include excessive tearing and tear staining (may be light pink or a rusty brown in color). This is partly due to the fact that

Shih Tzu have round eyes, which spill the tears over the rim of the eye rather than letting them flow to the corner of the eye and down the tear duct. However, some Shih Tzu never experience eye stain, which is a mystery.

There are many possible reasons for excessive tearing and tear staining. They include:

- Eye disease (can cause blindness)
- Blocked or very small tear ducts
- Extra row of eyelashes
- Eyelids that turn inward
- Eye infection
- Allergies
- Teething (puppies)
- Excessive amounts of iron in the diet or water

If your Shih Tzu experiences excessive tearing or staining, talk to your vet about possible options for fixing the problem. Remember that staining varies from dog to dog. Some experience it more extensively than others do, but it is treatable in most cases.

If it is a case of very small or blocked tear duct, the vet can perform a simple test where he will put a little stain into the eyes to color the tears, and then he'll watch how the eyes drain towards the nose. If the stain doesn't show up there, he knows the duct is blocked and can prescribe proper treatment.

If your Shih Tzu suffers from allergies, the good news is that the tearing and staining will only be seasonal and the dog's allergies can be treated properly by the vet or it may clear up on its own with no treatment needed.

There isn't a single cause or solution to this problem. It needs to be looked at on a case by case basis. Treatments are available to help clear up the problem unless it is a more serious type of eye affliction that requires special treatment.

If the tearing and staining are not caused by a more serious condition, you can treat the problem cosmetically by doing the following:

- Keep the face clean
  - Clean the hair under the eye several times a month with a mild shampoo. (Use the shampoo recipe in this book) or use a diluted solution of lemon juice mixed with a little salt. The pet store will also sell a salt solution already mixed that you can use
  - **NEVER** put any drops or ointment into the eye without a prescription from the vet
  - Buy one of the many products available that when placed under the eyes allow the tears to flow over it without staining the face. Vaseline will do the trick as well
- Keep the hair around the eyes trimmed

Remember that the first thing that needs to be done is to determine the cause of the tearing or staining. All types of problems need to first be ruled out before you try to treat the problem yourself. If the eyes are healthy, then it is only a matter of cosmetics, which can easily be fixed.

As a side note, there is some interesting research available on canine cataracts of the eye at: http://www.heartbreeders.org/heart/genetics.htm, go there and read about it.

Professional Veterinary Care

The Right Vet for Your Dog

There will certainly be times when home treatments for certain conditions will not solve the health issues with your Shih Tzu. It's times like that when you will need to seek the care and advice of a qualified veterinarian.

If you don't already have a vet, you need to search for one that you will feel comfortable with. It is not an easy decision to entrust the care of your beloved Shih Tzu to someone you don't know.

First of all, here are several things you should **NEVER** use as criteria for choosing a vet.

- How friendly he is
- How close his office is to your house
- How much his office staff coos over your dog

The truth of the matter is that it is the philosophy of the vet that counts!

Let me explain. There are two different philosophies in veterinary medicine.

1. The American Veterinary Medical Association (AVMA) represents the "allopathic" philosophy (western or conventional medicine).
2. The American Holistic Veterinary Medical Association (AHVMA) represents the "holistic" philosophy (natural medicine).

The holistic medical practice is growing **VERY** fast, as more vets realize its enormous advantages.

Allopathic Medicine

The allopathic philosophy of veterinary medicine is based on the following:

- Drugs
- Medications
- Chemicals

Vets who practice this kind of medicine will treat any condition that your dog may encounter with drugs, medicines or other chemicals. While some of these methods, for instance, medicines may do some good, others like chemicals can cause the dog's body a great deal of stress.

Sometimes the body doesn't respond to the presence of foreign substances well and may have some type of reaction. In some cases, the dog's immune system will also put up a fight against these substances, trying to rid their bodies of it. This type of stress on the body can take a toll by forcing the immune system to fight the substances while it is trying to fight the illness as well.

In addition to this stress, there are possible side affects with these substances, which in turn are treated with more drugs, medications or chemicals. It's a viscous circle.

Here is what a qualified Veterinarian had to say on the subject. Dr. Richard

Pitcairn D.V.M. says, "In our eagerness for quick and easy solutions, we seize on a certain drug that may just cover up symptoms without addressing underlying causes. For example, synthetic cortisone is powerful enough to stop a wide variety of symptoms in their tracks, but inside, the disturbance continues unseen. Animals vigorously treated with such drugs (apparently successfully) go on to develop another condition within a few weeks or months. The suppressed disorder has simply gone on to create more serious inroads in the body."

Holistic Medicine

The holistic philosophy of veterinary medicine is based on the following:

- Safety,
- Sensibility
- Moderation

This type of veterinary medicine is gaining in popularity in the US as more and more dog owners recognize the benefits. Since the word holistic is derived from the word “whole”, the philosophy of this medical practice focuses on the **WHOLE** dog (body, mind, spirit and environment).

Vets that practice holistic medicine take the approach of building the immune system to resist disease and prevent contraction of it. They firmly believe that it is best to promote wellness from the inside out. If the dog does experience a health problem, they then will boost the immune system even more by the use of medicinal herbs, nutritional supplements, vitamins and minerals, enzymes and antioxidants, chiropractic care, acupuncture, homeopathy and just plain common sense support and care.

They believe in using the simplest, safest and most gentle methods that will produce results without adverse affects. They will however use conventional methods of treatment such as steroids, antibiotics, medications, drugs and chemicals **ONLY** when nothing else they try works.

It is important to point out that holistic vets are qualified to practice both allopathic and holistic medicine. They go to the same veterinary schools and get the same type of licenses as other vets. What makes them different is that they also train in natural treatments as well. So basically you get the best of both options when you choose a holistic vet for your dog's care.
Look in your local yellow pages for both allopathic and holistic vets or search on line. You can find a list of holistic vets at: http://www.shirleys-wellness-cafe.com/vetlist.htm and http://www.viim.org/findvets/vetlist.asp
You can find allopathic (conventional) vets in your local area.

Your Dog's First Vet Visit

It might help to know what you could expect when you take your Shih Tzu to the vet for the first time. First of all, you will have to be firm with the dog and act like it's no big deal, that it is a great trip that you are making together. The reason for this is that if you try to soothe the dog, he will think you are praising him. When he is shaking half scared to death, he will think that is how he should act when you go to the vet. So you need to take the action of being "matter of fact: about the whole thing.

You can help him overcome his fright by letting him get use to the waiting room and let the office help pet him or give him a treat. Whatever you do, don't let him get near the other dogs, this will add to his anxiety. I know this may be hard to do, but you have to do it.

If your Shih Tzu likes to be groomed, then bring a brush along to keep his mind occupied. It may sooth him since he loves being groomed anyway. You can also divert his attention by pretending not to notice how nervous he is and having him sit or lie down. He'll get the message that it's no big deal.

When you are called in to see the vet, don't focus your attention on the dog when he is being examined. If the dog is behaving well during the examination, reward him with a treat. If on the other hand, the dog is behaving badly, hold him firmly but cheerfully chat with the vet. This sends the message that you are in control but you are ignoring the bad behavior. If you try these little tricks when you go to the vet, eventually the dog will get the idea that it's not so bad after all.

Vaccinations

According to veterinary researchers, yearly vaccinations are not necessary as a means of prevention because many vaccines have little or no effect on preventing diseases. They further recommend that only core vaccines be administered. Other types of vaccines should only be given on an "as needed" basis determined by your vet based on tests run on the dog (blood titers). Blood titers are used as a means of determining the level of antibodies present in the blood to protect the animal against disease. This test will also help the vet to determine if vaccinations are necessary at all. Some states do require yearly vaccination by law, while others require the immunization be given every 3 years.

The thing to remember about vaccines is that they are not given to prevent disease; in fact they are the disease that is being given to the dog. The vaccine is a diluted version of the disease it represents such as distemper. When the dog receives the vaccine, his immune system is suppose to go to work to form antibodies to build an immunity to that particular disease. It is actually the dog's immune system that protects him from disease.

Here's what a qualified vet has to say about vaccinations. Dr. Christina Chambreau D.V.M. says, "Would you rebel if your doctor told you to have measles, mumps, rubella, diphtheria, pertussis, tetanus, and hepatitis shots every year of your life until you died, instead of only a few doses as a child? People don't need yearly re-vaccinations. Now veterinarians and immunological researchers tell us: Neither do dogs and cats."

Keeping Your Shih Tzu Healthy

Health Problems of Shih Tzu

The simple truth is that prevention is the key to keeping your Shih Tzu Healthy. There are several diseases that Shih Tzu are prone to and can occur often. They include:

- Allergies (skin problems)
- Bladder stones
- Weak knee joints
- Dental (tartar and early tooth loss)
- Eye disease
- Ear infections
- Endocrine system disease
- Seizures

Although they are not prone to gum disease (gingivitis), if they experience this condition, it can spread to the kidneys, liver or heart and can kill the dog if not treated correctly.

Shih Tzu are also known to have other health problems including weepy eyes, blocked tear ducts, skin problems, and epilepsy (seizures). There are also many illnesses and diseases though not necessarily afflicting only Shih Tzu, but canines in general, that you need to be aware of. Some of these diseases can be genetic. Many will be discussed in this section.

Various Types of Illnesses

If your Shih Tzu is in good health and contracts cataracts in his eyes, they can be successfully removed but cannot be fully cured. You can also opt to have one eye at a time done to minimize his incapacitation and discomfort. Diseases of the heart such as heart murmurs and more serious types of heart disease can occur. Monitoring and treatment by your vet is the best thing you can do in this case.

You need to constantly be aware in any changes in the dog's behavior or routine. They can be early indications of potentially serious health problems brewing. Diseases of the endocrine system such as Diabetes and Cushings Syndrome could occur, so the earlier that you notice the symptoms, the earlier your dog can receive treatment that may save his life.

Also, if the dog has seizures, immediate testing to determine the underlying cause is vital to determine the proper course of treatment. Early detection and treatment of parasite and flea problems is also key to early treatment and control of these pests.

You can also keep your Shih Tzu healthy by spaying or neutering him/her early in life. It is important that this be done early in the dog's life to prevent mammary cancer in the female or prostate cancer in the male. The Veterinary Cancer Society lists the following ten common signs of cancer in small animals:

1. Abnormal swellings that persist or continue to grow
2. Sores that do not heal
3. Weight loss
4. Loss of appetite

5. Bleeding or discharge from any body opening
6. Offensive odor
7. Difficult eating or swallowing
8. Hesitation to exercise or loss of stamina
9. Persistent lameness or stiffness
10. Difficult breathing, urinating or defecating

Another health issue facing Shih Tzu is the possibility of their windpipe (trachea) collapsing. This can be a potentially dangerous situation. The problem is due to the weakening of the windpipe, which then collapses, cutting off the ability to breathe properly.

There are warning signs that you should be aware of. If you hear clicking sounds coming for the dog's throat or if the dog is choking and showing signs of breathing difficulties, take him to the vet immediately. These could be indications of a collapsed windpipe and this should be considered an emergency situation.

Some Shih Tzu can have an "autoimmune" condition called "immotile cilia syndrome" (or Kartagener's syndrome). It may mimic pneumonia, kennel cough or distemper and causes the dogs to have multiple symptoms. Symptoms may include:

- Frequent respiratory disease
- Excessively runny nose
- Difficulty overcoming infections

It is important to note that this condition is probably hereditary.

Bladder Stones

Some Shih Tzu have a predisposition to developing kidney stones or bladder stones. Several different types of stones may form in the bladder including calcium stones, magnesium phosphate stones or infection stones. The best way to help prevent the formation of bladder stones is to make sure to provide your Shih Tzu with plenty of fresh drinking water at all times. However, if your Shih Tzu happens to be predisposed to developing stones, you will need to have him treated by the vet.

Renal Dysplasia

The always fatal kidney disease known as renal dysplasia is common in all breeds of dogs (by some estimates, after the age of eight as many as 85 percent of all dogs will have some kidney degeneration), however, it is even more common in Shih Tzu than in the average dog.

The condition may be inherited because often more than one puppy from the same litter, or even the entire litter, will be affected. Responsible breeders will not breed animals whose offspring have exhibited this trait.

The disease has three stages, and unfortunately no symptoms appear until the second stage. The disease may progress over months or years to reach the point where symptoms become obvious.

Dogs with renal dysplasia will become excessively thirsty and will pass large amounts of diluted urine. They may lack energy and suffer from a poor appetite. In the last stage of the disease, the symptoms become more severe and may include diarrhea, dehydration and vomiting. There is no cure at the present time.

Kidney Stones

Male dogs, like male humans, are more prone to kidney and bladder stones because of their narrower urethras that are more easily clogged. Urate stones are composed of uric acid and occur more often in the males' urinary tract when the urine is acid. Another kind of stone is the cystine urolith, an inherited condition which is made up of the aminor acid cystine. These account for about five percent of stones and are found only in males.
Such stones require surgery to remove.

However, phosphate stones—which are associated with alkaline urine and often with a bladder infection—are the most common kind of stones, and they are found more often in females. Therefore, simply selecting a female dog is no insurance against stones.

Hot Spots

"Hot spots" are surface skin infections caused when populations of normal skin bacteria grow and overwhelm normal resistance. They are generally circular patches that lose hair, can be swollen, in extreme cases may exude smelly pus, and can be painfully itchy causing the dog to scratch, lick, or bite to
the point of self mutilation. Untreated hot spots can spread and provoke a normally even-tempered dog to growl or nip when touched.

Dogs most susceptible to hot spots are those with heavy coats and histories

of allergies, ear infections, flea infestations, irritated anal sacs and grooming problems such as hair tangles and mats. The most common location for hot spots is the legs, feet, flanks and rump. These localized infections can also appear on the ears, neck, and chest if the dog is continually scratching.
To treat hot spots trim the hair around the sore to prevent further spread of the infection and expose the edges of the lesion. Wash the area in a mild water-based astringent or antiseptic. There are over-the-counter products to deter the dog from licking and chewing. The #1 product for most breeders and handlers is called "tea tree spray" or melaluca alternifolia. It is supposed to have healing qualities as well as discouraging the dog from biting or licking himself due to the bad taste.

I also use a product called ***Sulfodene*** which is specifically for hot spots. I have had good results with this and it can be purchased almost anywhere that sells pet products. (Department stores, grocery stores, etc.)

If treated early hot spots may disappear in day or two. Sulfodene is a good early treatment product. Or, try medicated powder. Dust the spot several times a day to dry any moisture and soothe the itch. This can also be purchased over-the-counter.

Creams and ointments are not recommended because they can seal in the infection and hinder recovery. Although, a prescribed ointment may be necessary if the area becomes infected.

At this stage the hot spot needs to checked by a veterinarian for treatment. Some pet owners demand a quick fix for the problem and aren't tolerant of vets who require return visits. Some vets will give you that quick fix by prescribing steroids for allergies. This quick fix is called "Prednisone". However, you are setting your Shih Tzu up for serious problems later in life if you do this repeatedly. **If you use the Prednisone do so sparingly**. Once or twice a month during allergy season followed by antihistamines. A steroid given over and over can affect the balance of cortisol in the dog resulting in a condition called "Cushings Syndrome".

Our oldest Shih Tzu developed hot spots that got to the point of needing vet care. Our vet had just retired so we used the vet that took over for him. He gave us medications for her and also put the ***dreaded*** e-collar on her. She was miserable, running into the walls; she couldn't get thru the doggie door, etc.

I didn't know just how miserable she was until the second night. She got in bed with us and just whined, she never slept with us so this spoke **volumes**. I got up around midnight and took her into the dining room so I wouldn't wake my husband.
I told her I would take the head gear off if she promised not to scratch or bite. (Obviously, she agreed). I took the e-collar off and put it on a high shelf in the basement. ***She never once touched the hot-spot and it healed fine.***

I went to the basement a few days later, and found the e-collar on the floor! I don't know how she reached it, unless she stood on our Border Collies' back, but that e-collar was chewed to pieces. ***(I love dogs!)***

Needless to say we changed vets. The new vet said he would have only used the e-collar as a last resort. So, once again, **be careful of the vet you choose**.

Endocrine System

Endocrine system disorders occur more frequently in Shih Tzu than you would think. Often enough that it is worth making you aware of these conditions so that you can get the dog properly diagnosed and treated as early as possible.

It is because of the working relationship of the secretions of the endocrine glands. If the system breaks down in any way, it can result in ill health that is life threatening. The good news is that they are all treatable illnesses and the sooner found the better.

Basically four types of endocrine illnesses can occur in Shih Tzu. They include:

- Pancreatitis
- Diabetes
- Cushing's disease (or Cushing's Syndrome)
- Hypothyroidism

You should also know that most of these illnesses are appearing in older Shih Tzu but some younger Shih Tzu have also showed signs of them. Additionally, it seems that once one of these conditions has been diagnosed, it appears that there is a good chance that one of the others will develop eventually.

There are many things that you can do to prevent the onset of these illnesses. First and foremost, as stated earlier, a good nutritional balanced diet, moderate exercise and fresh drinking water will go a long way in helping to keep your Shih Tzu healthy.

Preventive measures such as early detection of problems, regular veterinary checkups and vaccinations (core vaccines only) will also help. Core vaccinations include those for distemper, parvo, adenovirus and rabies. Make sure to wait about a month after a rabies shot to have other vaccines given to the dog.

If you are constantly observant, especially when grooming the dog, you will have a better chance of noticing any physical changes in your dog or his habits and you can take swift action possibly avoiding a potential crisis.

Remember that your dog can't watch out for himself. He looks to his caretakers to take the very best care of him and his needs. In return, you will have a happier and certainly healthier companion.

Exercise

The American Animal Hospital Association (AAHA) suggests that you also start your pet on a daily exercise routine. While Shih Tzu don't require a **lot** of exercise because they enjoy dashing around the house, they should have some sort of scheduled exercise time.

You can plan something as simple as a daily walk with you or frolic around in the yard. You don't want to limit the exercise time to the weekends because this can do more harm than good and it could lead to orthopedic injuries occurring.

On the other hand, don't over do it or other problems may arise down the road, like arthritis setting in.

Remember that Shih Tzu are naturally energetic so a little scheduled exercise (10-15 minutes daily) will go along way. A good walk or run daily should do it and make your Shih Tzu a whole lot healthier in the process.

Differences Between Show and Pet Quality

You already know that all Shih Tzu can be raised as pets, but not all can be raised as show dogs. The reason for this is because the AKC standards clearly spell out what is required as far as characteristics go to determine if a Shih Tzu is of show quality. Every owner who is raising his Shih Tzu as a show dog must have the dog's characteristics match the AKC standard.

So just how would you determine if your Shih Tzu has what it takes to become a show dog? Well, answer the following questions honestly and if you answer yes to all of these questions, seek an evaluation of your Shih Tzu by a reputable handler for possible show competitions.

1. Temperament: Does your Shih Tzu have a friendly and outgoing personality to everyone, not just you?

2. Attitude: Does your Shih Tzu have a "here I am, you got to love me attitude?"

3. Size: Is your Shih Tzu 9 ½ inches or more but less than 12 inches?

4. Eyes: Are the eyes black/dark?

5. Pigment: Are the lips, pads and nose black?

6. Bite: Does he/she have a scissors bite?

7. Halos: Is there black or dark skin surrounding the eyes?

8. Proportions: Does he/she match the AKC standard proportions?

9. Movement: Have an expert evaluate this because it is too difficult for you to determine on your own.

Training Tips

While a library of books could not contain all the good advice available to dog owners, here are a few tips that might be helpful for you and your Shih Tzu.

My Shih Tzu likes to nip at me when sitting on my lap or playing.

Use your most powerful training tool to stop this and other unacceptable behavior—your stern disapproval. Without fail, even when it doesn't hurt, remove your Shih Tzu from your lap or leave him and go into another room every time he bites. Don't yell or wag a finger at him as he will interpret this as attention from you and you'll just be reinforcing the bad behavior. Smacking him on his sensitive nose won't work either, as it will just encourage him to be aggressive because you are actually modeling the type of behavior you want to discourage. But don't stay "mad" long. As soon as your Shih Tzu comes to you for comfort after this terrible snub, give him your full attention and praise when he is not biting. He will soon learn to connect his biting with your disapproval.

My Shih Tzu chews on everything in the house!

Look at your home from your dog's perspective and you will see it is filled with an endless variety of satisfying chewing textures and opportunities. You can't expect your little friend to know the difference between a rawhide chew toy and a pair of Italian leather shoes. Try to keep objects that might tempt her in closets or otherwise out of reach. Whenever she starts gnawing on a forbidden item, remove it immediately and tell her "No, no!" in your most disapproving voice. Then give her an approved chewing object (always keep a variety of safe chewing toys on hand) and praise her when she chews it. She will soon learn to prefer her approved chew toys because they lead to praise instead of scolding.

Remember that young dogs cut their adult teeth just like human babies, and they need to spend a lot of time chewing. It is also a healthy activity for their teeth and gums.

It's not a good idea to give your Shih Tzu an old shoe to chew, as she may not be able to distinguish the approved shoe from other shoes in the household. Pet stores have whole aisles of safe chew toys to keep your dog happy and safe.

Be sure to remove any chew toy that is coming apart and may become unsafe if your Shih Tzu swallows small pieces.

Is an obedience class a good idea for my Shih Tzu?

Pet owners have widely varying opinions on this subject, and you will have to decide for yourself whether an obedience class is a good idea for you and your individual Shih Tzu.

Some people think such classes rely too heavily on treat rewards (which might not be a good idea for a small dog that gains weight easily, like a Shih Tzu). They question whether such classes can be effective in training dogs away from the home environment in which they live. But many dog owners have found the classes to be extremely helpful.

Check out the classes that are available in your area. Find out what approach they take to training your dog. Finally, because a Shih Tzu is a small dog, be sure to enroll in a class for small dogs. You don't want your cherished friend to be traumatized by an aggressive large breed dog in the circle next to you.

Another alternative might be to hire the services of a professional dog trainer. Your vet can recommend an individual who can give you concrete, helpful suggestions tailored to your individual Shih Tzu and situation.

I worry about spoiling my Shih Tzu. But I don't want to be harsh and make her hate me. What attitude should I take when training my dog?

If you worry that humane methods such as using the expression in your voice or removing your attention from your dog are too cruel, think about it this way. A dog, like a child, needs limits to feel secure. You are the source of food and toys and all good things in your dog's life. She will feel secure if she feels you are in control. You need to be firm and consistent in training your little dog in the rules of the house. Don't feel apologetic. A spoiled, untrained dog is not a joy to anyone. Don't think of it as punishing your dog, but as training her. Also, her safety and her very life could depend on her being an obedient, well trained animal. For example, if she were chewing on an unsafe object, you would want her to easily allow you to remove it. If she escaped the yard, you would want her to come when called so she doesn't get run over. It may seem like tough love, but as long as you are using kind, gentle, human training methods you are doing your Shih Tzu and yourself a great favor in being consistent and firm in your training, especially in your early months together. The reward will be years of agreeable companionship.

HOW DO I GET MY DOG TO STOP EATING POOP???!!

I don't think there is any one way to get dogs to leave stool alone. Below are a few suggestions. You can try any or all of the below!

- The best help to curb poop eaters is to keep the stool as cleaned up as possible. I joke with people and tell them to teach their dog to poop in a shovel!
- There is a product available through your veterinarian called "For-Bid". It is an additive for the dog's food that supposedly will make the stool less desirable for them (as if it isn't already!).
- Some people have success with mixing meat tenderizer like Adolf's into the dog's food each meal. It is supposed to have the same effect as For-Bid.
- Accompany your dog outside each and every time, and teach and use a command such as "Leave It!" to get him to avoid stool.
- Your neighbors will wonder what you are doing with this one: go outside and sprinkle an ample quantity of Tabasco-type sauce on each and every stool. The sauce has to be very hot, because some dogs enjoy the more mild hot sauces.
- Spray a bitter apple, bitter orange or similar deterrent on each stool.
- For dogs who will turn around and eat their own stool as soon as they are finished, or for those who eat others' stool as they are pooping, the best way unfortunately is to have your dog on leash and use the "leave it" command.
- One of our customers had this problem so we checked out a lot of

information. One source said to add a couple of teaspoons of pineapple to the dog's food. When digested an enzyme is created that deters the dog.

Pros and Cons of Raising Shih Tzu

Like most small dogs, Shih Tzu have a long lifespan, from 11 to 15 years with individuals sometimes living longer. You will want to be alert for possible health problems that could lesson their life spans considerably.

Like all breeds, Shih Tzu are more prone to certain specific health problems than other dogs. This section describes some of these possible health issues, but remember that even though these problems are more common in Shih Tzu than some other breeds, chances are that your dog, if acquired from a reputable breeder, will never have these problems. They are simply issues to be aware of.

- In general, some Shih Tzu tend to have ear and respiratory problems. They may wheeze and snore, however, this could be due to their short muzzles as much as to respiratory infections.

- Their long backs in relation to their short legs can lead to spinal disc disease, and they can have slipped stifles (the joint in a dog’s hind legs that corresponds to the human kneecap).

- You will want to give their teeth special attention as this breed can be prone to losing them early.

- Your vet may recommend an eye wash to use daily to keep your Shih Tzu’s eyes free of the dust and dirt that so often finds its way into the eyes of small dogs whose faces are so close to the ground.

- Shih Tzu can be sensitive to the heat, another fact you'll want to bear in mind when considering adopting a Shih Tzu.

- Shih Tzu are active dogs but can do well in an apartment, although they also enjoy larger spaces. They gain weight easily and may become overweight, a dangerous health condition. Carefully feed your Shih Tzu the recommended amount of food and see that she gets daily exercise, whether chasing a ball in the living room or going for a walk, to keep her fit and healthy and happy.

- Shih Tzu shed very little hair. If you keep your dog well groomed, she will lose little skin dander, making the Shih Tzu a good choice for someone with mild dog allergies. You will also want to keep your Shih Tzu well groomed to avoid skin problems such as infections and hot spots, as well as lesser problems such as mats and tangles. For this reason, you should select another breed if you don't have the time to groom your Shih Tzu at least once every other day (daily is preferable). Keeping your Shih Tzu well groomed will prevent a whole host of difficult-to-solve problems.

Breeding Your Shih Tzu

The big question for any purebred dog owner is whether or not to breed the dog. It basically comes down to a matter of preference. If you want to breed Shih Tzus and your dog can pass the following criteria for breeding, then by all means go ahead and give it a try.

You may consider breeding your Shih Tzu if:

- The dog is healthy and certified (OFA, CERF) to be free of genetic disease and came from parents and grandparents who were also certified.
- The dog fits the standard well enough to be awarded points at a dog show under respected judges.
- The dog has a stable temperament, meaning it is not shy as well as not aggressive.
- The dog has at least four titled dogs (conformation. obedience, tracking, agility, etc.) in the last three generations.
- You should have a minimum of a five-generation pedigree on your dog and are aware of any health problems in those five generations.
- You must be prepared to cover the costs of veterinary care for the mother before and after the birth. Also that you will care for the puppies, including veterinary care, for at least 10 weeks or longer. This includes preliminary house training and the first two sets of shots, early grooming, coat care and early teething.

You may not consider breeding Shih Tzus because:

- You don't have adequate room for mom and pups to be in a quiet indoor place during and after birth.

- You don't have the money to prepare for emergency care that may arise before or during birth or with the puppies in the critical weeks after they are born.

- You don't have any information on the health of previous generations. This applies to the father (sire) of the puppies as well as the mother (dam or bitch).
- You are looking to get rich quick! You should be aware that most breeders who provide the proper care find they often lose money instead of making money. If they are lucky, they may break even. If they are unlucky, they may not only lose money but may also lose a beloved pet when they find too late that she was not a good breeding prospect.

The fact is that breeding should be done to improve the breed and this can only be done by possessing knowledge about the breed and about your particular pet. Be sure that your motives are the right ones before jumping into breeding. If you don't plan to breed your Shih Tzu, it is best to have them neutered and spayed for the health of your pet and for the breed. It is a fact that neutered animals live longer and are more likely to be free of cancer and other life-threatening diseases?

To breed Shih Tzus, Health is Important

If you plan to breed your Shih Tzu, health is a major consideration. You must at a minimum have your Shih Tzu checked for the following and given a clean bill of health before you go ahead with the breeding. Now, having said that, I will add that breeding can be a very rewarding experience. My husband and I enjoyed it very much, and it was a great

experience for our children, grandchildren and our friend's children. We were once told by one of our customers "You have the best job in the world because you make people happy." We have carried that with us ever since.

Overall Health

- Fully examined and appears to be healthy
- Eyes examined and clear of any diseases as evidenced by CERF certificates
- Hips examined and clear of hip dysplasia as evidenced by OFA certificates
- Patellas examined and appears to be clear of luxation as evidenced by OFA certificates
- Hearts examined and appears to be clear of any diseases

Temperament

Shih Tzus who appear to have healthy, happy temperaments and who do not appear to be aggressive, overly shy, or otherwise abnormal.

Standard

Shih Tzus who appear to conform to the guidelines and be within the limitations of the Official Standard for the Shih Tzu as determined/recognized by the Shih Tzu Club of America and the American Kennel Club.

Registration

Always stick with AKC registered Shih Tzus! There have been some other "registrations" that have cropped up but they are not reputable! AKC requires DNA testing where other kennel clubs don't so the puppy mills usually go with another club. They usually don't know which male bred which female because they have a lot of studs and females, so buyer beware.

Personal Appearance Preferences

Personal appearance preferences within the standard should guide your breeding program. Your Shih Tzu should have reasonably good movement, beautiful head, reasonable length of neck, and whose size falls somewhere between 10.5 and 11 inches at the withers.

Frequency of Breeding

It is best to not breed the dog too often. Shih Tzus come in "heat" once every six months. They're pregnant for two months, and the puppies nurse for about four weeks before they can be weened. The mother needs time to heal and recover between litters. I recommend breeding once a year, and never breed more than 3 times over a two year period.

A female Shih Tzu may come into “heat” as early as six months of age. And about every six months thereafter. Speak with your vet before you decide to breed to determine if your Shih Tzu is a good candidate for breeding.

If you do decide to breed your Shih Tzu, you should wait until her second or third season.

Plan to breed about six and a half months after the start of her last season. Take some time to find a good stud. As with finding a good puppy, the same holds true when finding a good stud. Use the same care and guidelines. A good stud should complement any bad traits found in the female. Stud fees generally tend to run in the range of the cost of a puppy. It is not uncommon for the stud provider to take the “pick of the litter” in exchange for services. The female will be ready to breed about twelve days after the first colored discharge appears. If possible make arrangements to board her with owner of the stud for a few days to insure she is there at the proper time. By the second day of a colored discharge, and for three days thereafter she should be ready to mate and conceive.

Be sure and keep her separate from all other male dogs for at least another week.

It is possible for be impregnated again.

The general gestation period, (the length of the pregnancy) is 61 – 63 days. Depending on the dog, she may need her diet altered to gain or lose weight. Consult your vet as to her feeding and nutritional needs.

Normally, she will need more food and possibly nutritional supplements for her and the puppies growing inside her.

Once the dam is pregnant and it is time to deliver the pups, a whelping pen can be easily and cheaply built. My husband made a simple one from 1"x12" wood and pegboard. Only the mother needs to be able to get out, not the puppies, so make sure to provide this access for the mom. If you don't want to try your hand at building a whelping pen, you can buy one on the Internet at places such as http://www.whelping-box.com/ or follow these instructions to try and make your own.

This is a very simple one to build but will serve the purpose well.

- Use 2 1"x12"x8's and a 4'x8' sheet of pegboard cut in half length-wise (2 4'x4' pieces). (Pegboard has holes so it provided some air-flow).
- Screw them together using the pegboards for the ends and the 1"x12" s for the sides. To create a 4'x8' pen.
- Use some old comforters and some old blankets as well as a sheet of heavy plastic large enough to cover the bottom of the pen. About 5'x10'.
- Put one of the comforters down first, next the plastic, another comforter then and place the pen on top.
- Put a couple more blankets or comforters down for padding.

Buy a small step-stool about 6" high for the mother to be able to get out but not the puppies. That's all there is to it. We found it worked well, was lightweight, and easy to clean and cheap. We also used the yard gates a couple of times and found this worked fine as well. Just make sure mama can get out because she needs a break occasionally.

Caring for Shih Tzu Pups

As I said earlier, my mother, sisters and I have been breeding and raising Shih Tzus for a long time. Between the 4 of us we have 56 years of combined experience. It has been our experience with the pups that most breeders don't get is that Shih Tzu puppies need interaction with children and adults from the beginning so they can interact with anyone without being aggressive.

As for caring for the pups, they need to be kept warm. (about 90 degrees) We used a heat lamp, and/or electric heater in the room.

If the litter is large (say 6-8 pups) you need to monitor the feeding and rotate the pups with the mother. We sometimes added powdered puppies milk to the mother's food to make the milk richer, particularly with larger litters. Our first Shih Tzu was given to us by my mother and she had extremely large litters, she had 10 pups one time and not enough milk so we bought a product that supplemented the mother's milk. We had to get up every hour or two to feed the babies, it wasn't easy but we had to do it. It may not be needed with smaller litters (2-4 pups).

Keep a supply of puppy formula on hand for emergency feedings or later weaning. You can also make a formula from evaporated milk, corn syrup, a little water and egg yolk.

A pet nurser kit is also a good idea to keep around. They available at most pet shops.

When the puppies are old enough (4-5 weeks) let them out of the pen to exercise. Not only is it good for the pups but there's not much better entertainment than watching a "herd" of puppies run around a room.

A Puppy's Temperment

A puppy's temperament is somewhat predetermined by the genes he/she inherits from parents and grandparents. A well-bred Shih Tzu pup should have a playful attitude and a trustful nature and should be happy and content if he/she is properly cared for. Even the best-tempered puppy can be ruined if he/she is not handled properly. If your pup was not born with perfect temperament there are some things that can be done about it. Take a look at the following things you should do to help create the right temperment.

- Make sure that you keep a pup with the litter and the Mom until between 10 and 13 weeks of age. This is to allow him to learn first to be a dog among other dogs, the key to finding his proper place in the world.
- During the time between 6 weeks and his departure to his new home, you will spend a lot of time socializing the pup and helping him learn to be a dog among humans.
- Expose him to people who come to visit, especially to children. A puppy may seem aloof when he first sees a new human. The human should get down on his level and let the pup come to him rather than to grab up the pup. This is especially true when the new human is a child. Sudden moves can be scary, even to a mild mannered puppy.
- Make him take walks on a lead and feel the grass under his feet.
- Let him have toys to play with and spend some time alone in his crate to learn to be without his family.
- Begin his house training and his natural instincts will teach him to keep his home unsoiled. (Here again, we had good success with traning

pads. We started the puppies on them almost immediately and found that by the time they went to their new homes, they mostly paper trained and ready for full housebreaking.)

Once the pups start leaving for new homes, stress to all new owners that they need to follow through on the lessons begun in your home. Exposure to new situations and new people will continue, probably throughout his life. It is up to the new owner to see to it that these are enjoyable experiences.

If the new owners have children, stress to them the need to teach them that the crate is the pup's private place and that a puppy that goes into the crate on his own to rest should be allowed to do so. A puppy must never be disturbed while he is eating and some owners may find it practical to place the puppy in the crate with the food bowl. This allows him to eat undisturbed and enhances his feeling that the crate is his personal den.

Contracts, Co-Ownership

You should probably consider selling the pups under contract on a co-ownership basis. Use your breeding guidelines and your discretion to determine which pups if any do not conform to your breeding standards and state in the contract that they must be spayed or neutered to prevent detriment to the breed. By using the contract method of selling you are accomplishing two objectives.

1. To maintain an interest in the dog. (And, thereby, having control of the breeding of the dog, and the selling of pups.)
2. To protect your reputation as a breeder

Advertising

If you advertise “puppies for sale" in a newspaper, national general dog magazine, or on an Internet site that "sells pets", be very careful who you sell to. Be as “picky” about your customer as they are about the pup. You could place an ad in a dog show catalog, or breed specific magazine, as the goal of this type of "advertising" is not to sell dogs, rather it is to provide Shih Tzu breed information and to hopefully help people in their search for information or a breeder.

Background

Never, ever buy a dog from a pet store or any backyard breeder. (By backyard breeder I mean someone who keeps the dogs penned in the yard and does not

socialize the dogs. These types of breeders do not care for their dogs and are often referred to as “puppy mills”.) Take your time to seek out a reputable breeder, wait if you have to, it will pay off in the long run. We sold a lot of puppies by word of mouth because our customers were always satisfied. I made sure of it and did follow up calls after a week and then again after a month. My customers always knew they could contact me with any questions.

Certificates and Pedigree Registrations

Some pet shops make a big deal out of their puppies' pedigrees.
This is interesting, as the pedigree is really just a piece of paper with names on it. Unless you know the dogs behind those names the pedigree is really quite useless to the new owner.

- Can the pet store tell you what your puppies grand- parents died of, or how long they lived?
- Do any of the dogs in your pup's pedigree carry genetic diseases?

Most pet store employees don't know any more about your puppy's background than you do.

A reputable breeder can tell you all of this information about your pup's family tree and more.
When you buy a puppy from a reputable breeder you're getting more than a piece of paper. You're getting the important information associated with the names too.

Many responsible breeders will achieve titles on their dogs by showing them under unbiased judges. They will achieve championships on their dogs, which tells that the dog is a good representation of the breed.

Some breeders also obtain obedience, or other titles that relate to the job that their breed of dog was originally bred to perform.
Many also achieve canine good citizen titles on their breeding dogs.
These titles will be shown on the dog's pedigree before and after the parents'

names. Ask the breeder to explain what the letters mean.

Tips For Dealing With Dog Emergencies

Have you ever thought about what you need to do should your dog – or another dog – ever suffer a serious, life-threatening injury? What if they have a severe allergy to an insect bite or a bee sting? It's great to know your vet's phone number, but what if something happens during off hours? What if you don't know where the closest emergency animal clinic is located?

Augh! Enough with the questions already, right? Any emergency is stressful and scary, and one involving that furry little four-legged member of your family is no exception. The toughest of owners can be instantly reduced to helpless balls of mush if something's wrong with their dogs and they can't figure out what to do.

1. Preparation is key.

The key to getting through a veterinary emergency is preparation. You may think you have that covered with a first aid kit and having the phone number to your vet handy, but what if there isn't enough time to move your dog? You need to be well-versed in some of the more common animal emergencies just in case a situation ever arises. And hey, if a situation never arises, you'll still feel more confident knowing that you have the ability to deal with one.

2. Know how to care for wounds.

Did you know that you shouldn't use hydrogen peroxide on a bleeding wound? Nope. It slows clotting to the area, which means your dog could actually lose more blood than he would if you didn't use the peroxide at all. In fact, the best way to treat a deep, severely bleeding wound is to apply a clean cloth and hold it in place for five minutes, and then tape the cloth to the wound. That original cloth should never be removed – that also slows clotting – and should instead be layered with more clean cloths if blood soaks through.

3. Know what to do about poisoning.

Did you know that certain varieties of toads, salamanders, newts, and other amphibians are poisonous if licked? Hey, guess who loves to hold little woodland critters in his mouth! Your dog.

If you notice your pup drooling, whining, and wiping at his mouth after a trip into the forest, get him to a clean water source and rinse his mouth thoroughly. While the poison can be fatal if left in the mouth, it's fairly easy to cleanse from the tongue and glands.

Now imagine all of the scenarios that can happen to your dog, from fractured limbs to choking and everything in between. Do you really want to risk not knowing how to handle them? You don't have to anymore, since I've written Secrets to a Healthy and Happy Pooch to help you learn how to cope with nearly any emergency as well as have the basis for handling all of the everyday and lifelong problems and situations you'll face with your dog. From choosing toys to cancer and everything in between, it's all in the book… as well as how to create the most effective first aid kit and handle the most common emergencies. Listen, even the most experienced dog owner needs a little help and advice now and then. Secrets to a Healthy and Happy Pooch are that constant source of help and advice.

Bonus Chapter 2

4 Things Frustrated Dog Owners Should Know

You've probably had a day or two when you felt like your dog just wasn't paying any attention to you at all, right? You talked, you yelled, you shouted, maybe you jumped up and down and waved your arms, but she just wasn't interested in anything you had to say to her in any tone of voice. You're not alone.

1. Your dog isn't human.

Unless you believe in pet psychics, there's really no way for you to read your pooch's mind and figure out exactly what she's thinking. The good news is that, like many dog owners, the problems you're having can probably be traced to one simple thing: you're trying to communicate with your dog from a human standpoint, and your dog isn't a human. Sure, you know that, but lots of humans try to relate with their dogs in the ways that they think are rational as humans. The problem is that dogs are driven in every act and every moment by very strong instincts. Deciphering those instincts and leveraging them to build a productive relationship is like finding the keys to the city.

2. Your dog doesn't speak English.

Take the word "no," for example. Does your dog speak English? Not understand English. Does she speak it? What's meaningful to her is your tone of voice, not the word itself. Now let's think about that – we're taking up excess time trying to teach our dog a word she'll never speak and that probably doesn't mean much to her anyway. Sure, it's meaningful to us, but that's only one side of the equation. What about something that's meaningful to both human and dog?

3. You know what a growl means, and your dog knows what a growl means.

If you think that mutually meaningful language doesn't exist, you're not thinking creatively enough. What does it say to you when a dog growls at you? Anything from "get away from my food" to "back off, dude," right? Yet in every case, a dog's growl typically means that she is not happy with whatever you've done. And you've seen dogs react to other dogs' growls, right? So you know what a growl means, and your dog knows what a growl means. Where's the disconnect? Growl at your dog!

No, seriously. The next time your pooch starts stepping outside her bounds or doing something you don't like, growl at her. A nice, strong, guttural growl that would put the alpha wolf in a pack to shame. While you're growling, look directly into her eyes. You're almost guaranteed that she'll back off.

Made in United States
Cleveland, OH
20 February 2025